Mousekin's fables have been adapted from the following Aesop's fables:

MOUSEKIN'S FABLES

Story and pictures by EDNA MILLER

Prentice-Hall, Inc.   Englewood Cliffs, N.J.

*For Eric, Melissa,
and Christopher*

Printed in the United States of America   • J

Prentice-Hall International, Inc., London
Prentice-Hall of Australia, Pty. Ltd., Sydney
Prentice-Hall Canada, Inc., Toronto
Prentice-Hall of India Private Ltd., New Delhi
Prentice Hall of Japan, Inc., Tokyo
Prentice-Hall of Southeast Asia Pte. Ltd., Singapore
Whitehall Books Limited, Wellington, New Zealand

10 9 8 7 6 5 4 3 2 1

Library of Congress Cataloging in Publication Data

Miller, Edna.
   Mousekin's fables.

   Summary: A retelling of Aesop's fables including
Mousekin and his woodland friends.
      1. Fables. [1. Fables] I. Title.
PZ8.2.M49Mo   [E]   82-7554
ISBN 0-13-604165-5   AACR2

Many creatures share Mousekin's home
in the woods.
Each has something to learn
from the other.
A white-footed mouse
must be quick to learn
a lesson each day in the forest.

January

A housecat strayed near the forest
and circled a frosty pond.
When it spied Mousekin nibbling weed grasses
that poked through the icy cover,
the cat crouched and crept silently
to the pond's frozen edge.

In one mighty leap, the housecat landed!

The thin cover of ice held Mousekin—
but not a well-fed cat!

LOOK...BEFORE YOU LEAP!

February

Mousekin awoke to a call of "bob-*WHITE*"
as a covey of quail settled down
for the night.
The bobwhites formed a circle
as they rested on the ground.
With tails toward the center
and each bird facing out,
they could watch for any danger
from above or below.
One bird ruffled its feathers and shoved.

Its neighbor shoved back and pecked hard.
Soon all the birds joined in the quarrel.
They flew in every direction.

A weasel watched the family scatter—
he took the plumpest one of all.

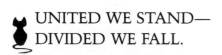 UNITED WE STAND—
DIVIDED WE FALL.

March

A wildcat kitten lived in the woods.
Mousekin had watched it play.
He had heard its mother's warning cry:
"Make no sound when left alone
unless you are in danger."
One evening while mother cat hunted food,
the kitten grew tired of play.
He wanted more excitement
than sticks and stones and old dried leaves.
The kitten screeched out loudly!

Mother cat bounded home to her den.
She found no danger there.
Each time the kitten played this game,
his mother rushed to his side.
One day she heard a screech and a squeal.
She wouldn't be tricked again!

She didn't see the large horned owl
swoop down from the wintry sky.

NO ONE BELIEVES A LIAR,
EVEN WHEN HE SPEAKS THE TRUTH.

April

A fox hunted food by a stream for her kits.
They were growing fast and always hungry.
Mousekin was hungry, too.
While busily searching beneath damp leaves
for tender shoots of green,
Mousekin found himself held fast
in the jaws of a large red fox.
The fox held Mousekin gently—
she wanted a live creature for her young.
As the fox crossed the stream,
she glanced into the water.
There she saw another fox
carrying a white-footed mouse.
How nice to have *two* live mice
to bring to her hungry ones!

As the fox snapped at her reflection
in the shallow water,
Mousekin dropped with a splash.

GRASP AT THE SHADOW
AND LOSE WHAT IS REAL.

A cottontail rabbit met a tortoise one day
and teased the slow-moving creature.
She hopped in circles all about him.
The tortoise stopped and pulled in his head.
"Though you may be quicker than I," he hissed,
"you would lose in a race with me."

"I'll race you to the pond," the rabbit called.
She was off before the tortoise
could stretch his neck to look around.

The rabbit, far ahead in the race,
stopped to nibble some blossoms and rest.
Mousekin watched the tortoise plod
past the sleeping cottontail.

SLOW BUT STEADY
WINS THE RACE.

June

A nuthatch and Mousekin shared seeds
that were wedged in the
craggy bark of a tree.
A hummingbird hovered on whirring wings
and watched the creatures feast.
"Come join the party," the nuthatch called,
as she split the seeds with
her stout pointed bill.
   The hummingbird tried again and again
   to pick up a bit of the food.
      His bill was too long and too slender.
      "ANK…ANK…ANK,"
         the nuthatch laughed.

"Come dine with me," the hummingbird squeaked.
Nuthatch and Mousekin hurried after.

With its long slender bill the hummingbird sipped
sweet nectar from a columbine blossom,
while two disappointed creatures watched
from a branch above.

 TREAT OTHERS AS YOU WOULD
HAVE THEM TREAT YOU.

July

A black bear found honey
inside a hollow tree.
Mousekin heard a scraping sound
as the bear reached in with his furry paw
to scoop the sweet stuff out.
The bear grunted and growled.
He wanted more honey, and faster.

With a swipe of his claws,
he ripped open the tree.
The swarm of bees flew out and away.
They would never return to that hollow tree.

DON'T BE GREEDY.

August

A large monarch butterfly came to rest
on a branch of an old birch tree.
At first it didn't see the moth
with its wings folded down,
looking just like the bark of the tree.
"How plain you are," the butterfly said,
fluttering her bright golden wings.
"If I hadn't come close,
I would never have known you were there!"

Mousekin gave a warning squeak
as a small hawk spied the golden wings
and dropped down from the sky.

BEING PLAIN HAS
ITS OWN REWARD.

September

A cold dew settled on the forest floor,
and a chilling breeze blew through the trees.
Mousekin knew it was time for him
to store his winter food.
As he stuffed his cheeks with seeds and nuts,
he heard a grasshopper sing:
"All days will be as bright as this,
all nights as warm and cheery."
The grasshopper stopped its merry chirp
when it saw Mousekin hard at work.
"What sort of creature are you
that you cannot stop to sing?"

Mousekin didn't answer—he had much to do—
for winter winds have little care
for those who will not store.

PREPARE TODAY FOR
THE NEEDS OF TOMORROW.

October

A hickory tree grew in the forest.
Its first fruit fell to the ground.
In autumn leaves beneath the tree,
Mousekin found a nut.
He carefully opened the thick green husk,
then split the paper-thin shell.
A chipmunk watched and waited
till the nutmeats dropped in two,
then scampered up to Mousekin
to take the food away.
As Mousekin rushed at the chipmunk
in a fury of nips and squeals,

a bluejay flew down from its perch above
and snatched away both pieces.

A HALF IS BETTER
THAN NONE AT ALL.

November

Mousekin heard foxes boasting
one cold and windy day.
"I can trick any hunter," one barked.
"I know every path through the forest, and
I can zig and zag and hide in a hundred places."
"I can do better than that," the other fox yapped.
"I can run like the wind,
then double back on my tracks to trick a foe."
Mousekin heard another sound—

the baying of hound dogs coming near.
The foxes rushed off in every direction.
Mousekin raced for the nearest tree.

BETTER ONE SURE WAY
THAN MANY HOPED FOR.

December

A deep snow covered the forest floor.
An icy wind rattled bare trees.
Mousekin tunneled beneath the snow
to find his stores of food.
When he came to the edge of the forest,
he stopped in his tracks to see
a tree with its branches filled with things
a mouse would want to eat.
There were strings of popcorn, red berries, nuts,
slices of apple, and seeds.

Beneath the tree the housecat sat.
He didn't want the food himself—
but chased each hungry creature coming near.

DON'T BE SELFISH.